This Book Belongs To:

MEZZO ZENTANGLE DESIGNS

MEZZO
ZENTANGLE
DESIGNS

MEZZO
ZENTANGLE
DESIGNS

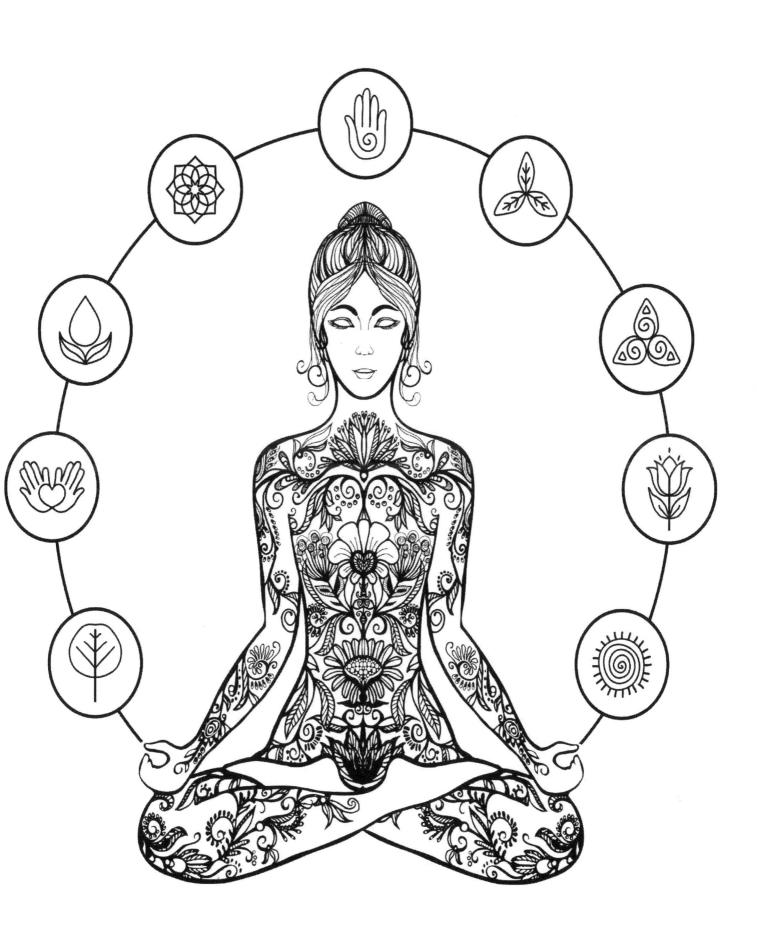

MEZZO
ZENTANGLE
DESIGNS

MEZZO
ZENTANGLE
DESIGNS

MEZZO
ZENTANGLE
DESIGNS

MEZZO
ZENTANGLE
DESIGNS

MEZZO
ZENTANGLE
DESIGNS

MEZZO
ZENTANGLE
DESIGNS

MEZZO
ZENTANGLE
DESIGNS

MEZZO
ZENTANGLE
DESIGNS

MEZZO
ZENTANGLE
DESIGNS

MEZZO
ZENTANGLE
DESIGNS

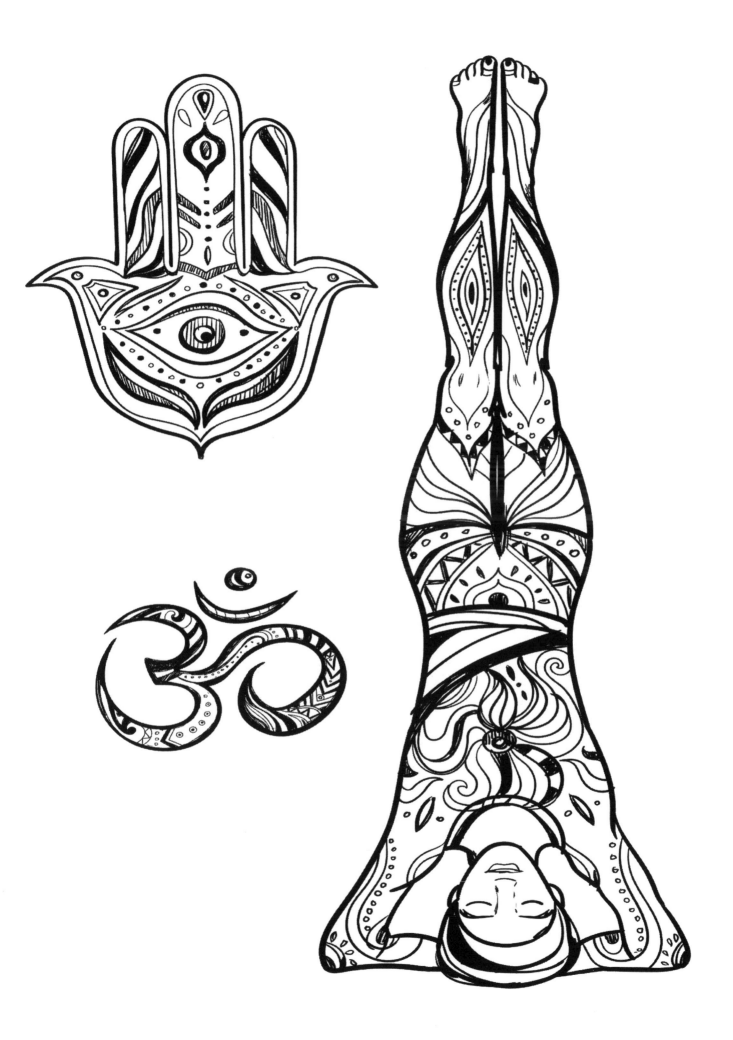

MEZZO
ZENTANGLE
DESIGNS

MEZZO
ZENTANGLE
DESIGNS

MEZZO
ZENTANGLE
DESIGNS

MEZZO
ZENTANGLE
DESIGNS

MEZZO
ZENTANGLE
DESIGNS

MEZZO
ZENTANGLE
DESIGNS

MEZZO
ZENTANGLE
DESIGNS

MEZZO
ZENTANGLE
DESIGNS

MEZZO
ZENTANGLE
DESIGNS

MEZZO
ZENTANGLE
DESIGNS

MEZZO
ZENTANGLE
DESIGNS

MEZZO
ZENTANGLE
DESIGNS

MEZZO
ZENTANGLE
DESIGNS

MEZZO
ZENTANGLE
DESIGNS

MEZZO
ZENTANGLE
DESIGNS

MEZZO
ZENTANGLE
DESIGNS

MEZZO
ZENTANGLE
DESIGNS

MEZZO
ZENTANGLE
DESIGNS

MEZZO
ZENTANGLE
DESIGNS

MEZZO
ZENTANGLE
DESIGNS

MEZZO
ZENTANGLE
DESIGNS

MEZZO
ZENTANGLE
DESIGNS

MEZZO
ZENTANGLE
DESIGNS

MEZZO
ZENTANGLE
DESIGNS

MEZZO
ZENTANGLE
DESIGNS

MEZZO
ZENTANGLE
DESIGNS

MEZZO
ZENTANGLE
DESIGNS

MEZZO
ZENTANGLE
DESIGNS

MEZZO
ZENTANGLE
DESIGNS

MEZZO
ZENTANGLE
DESIGNS

MEZZO
ZENTANGLE
DESIGNS

MEZZO
ZENTANGLE
DESIGNS

MEZZO
ZENTANGLE
DESIGNS

MEZZO
ZENTANGLE
DESIGNS

MEZZO
ZENTANGLE
DESIGNS

MEZZO
ZENTANGLE
DESIGNS

MEZZO
ZENTANGLE
DESIGNS

MEZZO
ZENTANGLE
DESIGNS

MEZZO
ZENTANGLE
DESIGNS

MEZZO
ZENTANGLE
DESIGNS

MEZZO
ZENTANGLE
DESIGNS

MEZZO
ZENTANGLE
DESIGNS

MEZZO
ZENTANGLE
DESIGNS

MEZZO
ZENTANGLE
DESIGNS

MEZZO
ZENTANGLE
DESIGNS

MEZZO
ZENTANGLE
DESIGNS

MEZZO
ZENTANGLE
DESIGNS

MEZZO
ZENTANGLE
DESIGNS

MEZZO
ZENTANGLE
DESIGNS

MEZZO
ZENTANGLE
DESIGNS

MEZZO
ZENTANGLE
DESIGNS

MEZZO
ZENTANGLE
DESIGNS

MEZZO
ZENTANGLE
DESIGNS

MEZZO
ZENTANGLE
DESIGNS

MEZZO
ZENTANGLE
DESIGNS

MEZZO
ZENTANGLE
DESIGNS

MEZZO
ZENTANGLE
DESIGNS

Printed in Great Britain
by Amazon